A Walk With You

James L. Mullen

JLMullen

Contents

A Walk With You

Seaside Dawn

As I rise in the morning
      A new day I see
And the joy of the Dawning
      Floods down over me.
I rejoice at the rising
      Of sun over sea
I rejoice at the countenance
      Smiling on me.
But the wind from the east
      Brings sensations anew
That enfold and caress me
      In all that I do.
I welcome the comfort
      Of the promise anew
And drink in its beauty
      As I always will do.

S

Something Slithers,
  Slides
Seeking Someone,
  Shy
Satin Sheets,
  Soft
Someone Sleeping,
  Saw
Seeking Shelter,
  Safe
Something Slipping,
  Stay
Suction Seizing,
  Stuck
Sweetly Swaying,
  Stops
Safety Shunning,
  Steps
Shyly Sighing,
  Sex

Blue Velvet

Blue Velvet Claws opening my shirt
Lovely Green Eyes possessing my own
Glinting Silver Fangs cooling my neck
the Breath of a Thousand Goddesses steaming my lens
  Enough for any man but all given to me
  Too much for mortal man, immortality my curse.
  I see death in her sweet-tasting lies
  Caressing my ego and drowning my self.

Sweet Night of My Innocence

Sweet Night of my innocence
Holy hour of my desire
Religion is, in a sense
Reality on fire

Tempting though it may be
Sweet Temptation of my soul
Damning me forever, maybe
With its burning of my soul

Lift me to the heights I see
Heights that always seem to grow
Bathe me in the vision icy
Frozen in the Holy Glow

Ice that burns in fiery lines
Define me with your chilling touch
Erase this heart that fire relines
Congeal my flame within your clutch

There's a Girl I Seem to See

There's a girl I seem to see
And the things she does to me
Make me sing in jubilee
of her sparkling majesty
Emerald eyes that shine so bright
Lighting up the darkest night
Focus me within their sight
Making everything seem right
Glowing lips of ruby red
Moving slowly in her head
Taking me with words unsaid
Down paths of thought not crossed as yet
Supple shoulders shaking softly
Caressed and steadied gently
Holding her in my arms closely
'Til no more she cries- then firmly
Grasping me within her arms
Holding me now safe from harm
Granting me without alarm
All I seek inside her charm
Then I turned from being led
Taking charge of her instead
Lying back upon the bed
"Take me now" was all she said
Softly stretched I o'er her
Softly laid myself upon her
Softly then I entered in her
Softly came and then I left her
Often dreams of this I see
Memories tangled up in me
Make me faint and feel so dizzy
Why I left her still a mystery

With Silent Lips

With silent lips unclosing
Her watery eyes gazed ceaselessly into mine
I lost all sense of motion
And stared— mesmerized—
into the depths of her cavernous soul
I was mortified by the uncertain size
And intrigued by the multitudinous shadows
hours upon hours, I stared— hopelessly lost.
Somehow I felt I was searching
Yet what I sought seemed to elude me.
Searing images of wonder and fear rose within my mind
Some were terrifying in their magnitude
Others lulled me with visions of paradise
yet the uncertainty of meaning remained
They were, to all ends, images only— and fleeting ones at that.
I searched for my soul, I felt—
and found it in flashes of indecipherable meaning.
She served as my mirror to my self.

Smiling Brightly She Turned

Smiling brightly she turned into reality
Shedding from unimaginable depths
Visions of perceived existence
Urgently intimating necessity
without requiring response
In full dread of what she could represent
I shrunk from her approach
and cowered lest she incinerate me

She simply advanced
passing quietly
Slipping majestically outward
While retaining inward attention
Expressly preventing all intervention
I felt the terror pass as she herself did
and watched in agony as she paused
turning to regard me in my pain

"What frightens you?"
her silken voice rubbed fiendishly on my soul of glass
"Can you not answer me?"
electrified her tortuous probe
I screamed inwardly in glorious pain
Melting in icy splinters of glass against my tender heart
I reached out to her and instantly caught flame
Maddened and exhilarated I lunged for more

Deftly she avoided my grasp
An apparition no longer present at the touch of desire
I hesitated and felt again the voice of her calling out to me

"Why do you seek the unattainable?"
I quivered in agony
"I can never be more than I seem,
and yet you are not content to look,"
imploded her query.

Dazed I stared and hoped for more
I looked for something corporeal to hold and saw nothing
I looked for something to own and saw nothing
I looked for something to feed on and saw nothing

A Walk With You

I looked for something to absorb and saw nothing
She was gone

I swallowed hard in despair
All my hope and selfish lusting was futile
Where once I felt the vibrant touch of love
I now saw dissipating mist,
and sorrowed at my loss.

I looked again, searching for any sign of her
and suffered anew at the absence
"NO!!!" I screamed into the void of my soul
"no," again and turned away at last
Noticing as I did a flutter in the corner of my eye
A brief glimpse of what was lost
Still present at the edge of my reality
And smiling brightly I turned…

Woods

Standing alone in the presence of greatness
Hidden amongst the towering pines
Safe and comfortable as the hours whisk by
Alone in the woods

The wind breathes through the branches stretching over my head
the occasional cluster of needles drops to the carpet around me
I lazily tread across the padded floor from tree to tree
gazing into their trunks, branches, leaves—
looking for their past and their souls
What I find escapes me—
lost instantaneously in the fathomless depth of the forest
I listen again for anything, and hear only the gentle laughter
of the wind in the pines.

As the day lengthens I head toward the small brook,
down the ledge, through the pines and tiny swamp.
I am drawn to its mysteries.

I gaze into the water, amazed at its clarity
No more than two feet wide the stream is equally deep
strewn at the bottom with tiny pebbles
gathered from the forest's heart.
A tiny waterfall is created by a dead tree branch lodged
in a pinched section
My feet lead me upstream along the trickling voice of passing time
Seeking the source of the swift brook's course

The path is rough—
As it meanders back and forth through outcrops of granite
and clusters of pine and spruce.
The underbrush thickens to a grasping menace,
hindering my progression upstream

With the suddenness of their arrival,
the difficulties guarding the path recede, and again
there is a sparsely populated canopy of pines in relative solitude
The underbrush has disappeared,
leaving the pines, the granite, the carpeted floor, and the stream.

Following the rippling water
I find myself faced with a choice at a juncture–
do I follow the dismal looking still-water contributor
back into its marsh,
or chase the life spark of the other rivulet
back up its dancing course down the sheet of granite

The choice is made
The cackling voice of the stream on the stone
draws me away from the muck of the marsh,
onwards and upwards over the treacherous, slippery rocks
The laughter of the cascade supplants the sarcastic ridicule
of the wind in the pines
Drawing me upstream with its enticing melodies.
I sense a need to hurry now,
I should be getting home, dinner will be ready,
my mother will fret over my absence
But I must wait a while longer,
I must find the source of the current which so stimulates my mind.
And so I continue up the stream
there is a ledge down which it has coursed,
creating a meandering waterfall
filled with rocks
and tiny pools of water.
Beyond this cascade,
the stream disappears into ever thicker underbrush
and low-hanging trees,
doubling back and forth on itself more frequently and more sharply.
My progress in locating the source of the stream is slowed
by the difficulty of passage posed by the enclosing woods.
Visibility has decreased, and I am constantly fighting my way
through violently grasping branches and soft marshy sod
along the streambed

Finally, I find what I have so desperately sought-
the source of this mesmerizing course-
In one sense I am disappointed,
I was enjoying the search, I was creating my own image
for the stream's source,
and now my attempts were contrasted with reality,
the differences stark in many aspects,
my own images somehow seeming more real to me-
the reality of the source wrong in some transcendental manner-

Yet, there was something mysterious-
something intriguing, something at once primeval, primordial,
about the bleak, dismal, sinister swamp-pond before me,
shrouded in silent, darkening mist,
a glimmering echo out of my unexperienced past
which came to me in a haunting image
of déjà-vu and sensory perception at more levels
than I thought humanly possible
Invoking my soul.

In the Cooling Shadows

In the cooling shadows of the evening
Alone before an iridescent sky
I waited silently for my true love
As the long minutes drifted slowly by
I heard a steady padding rising up
Above the gentle rhythm of the sea
I turned and looked into approaching eyes
That gazed across the sand with love on me
A voice reached forth from lips unto my ear
Caressing my mind with its subtle tongue
Dispelling cares and worries of the day
And promising my heart we would be one
Enveloped in each other's arms we watched
The sun sink slowly down beyond the sea
Until we were alone beneath the stars
Which stretched across the sky so carelessly
Hours drifted by in perfect harmony
Unfettered by desire or outright lust
In union we dreamed of future joys
Hoping in our hearts our jointure just
Time uncaring left us to our solace
The stars a silent partner in the night
The moon a chaperone to all our thoughts
Until the sun at dawn bathed us with light.
Awakened to a newfound love we rose
Together slipped away across the strand
Into forever we strode purposely
Side by side, heart to heart and hand in hand.

Trees & Grass

The wind stirs my soul
Like rustling leaves newly
dead to the forest floor

The sky draws my heart open
The grass caresses my legs
The earth lifts me solidly to the stars

I breathe deeply the air of freedom and love
The silent boughs stretch above me
Their watchful gaze
a comfort to my cares

Their arching branches an indifferent shelter to passing time
Happiness & Home
   —They permeate my mind

Lessons

Relax
Lay back in your loneliness
close your eyes & let the wind caress your face
Feel the sun warm your skin as you
picture the movement of the clouds across the sky in your mind
Listen to the trees–
They sing to each other, the earth & sky
They call out your dreams & aspirations to the universe
And mock you with their pleasantries.
But heed the wisdom of the earth
The understanding it offers based on millennia of existence.
Turn off your mind and relax
to nature's melody.

Sonnet 1

Behold! the lamb defying words of praise,
Who walks among the masses bringing peace,
Attracting also awe, and humbling gaze,
At beauty unrestrained and without cease-
She glows within from beauty of the soul
A vision of delight who stirs no lust,
Exuding and extracting thoughts so whole
That all are captured by her blessed trust-
Who can deny her power or her strength?
Which all hatred mocks as coarse and vain-
Which she in depth and weight and broadest length
Absolves, absorbing with her love all pain.
Around her shines her love, a shield from wrong-
Love unrestrained- beauty sheathed in song.

Sonnet 2

She smiled softly in her beauty brilliant
Divinely dressed in radiance unrefined
A jewel among rocks, unparalleled she stood
Aware of herself, but humbly restrained
Glowing without destroying the lifeline
Of the lesser glass bulbs that surround her
Jaw dropping stares unequally drawing
Admiration, commanding attention
While heightening the beauty of her peers
A diamond giving a golden luster
To lead settings, never felt out of place
Nor diminished in the least – yet she dims
By the bright light of her own emission
Burning out the confines of her own case

Sonnet 3

Look! She glows with radiance undiminished-
A star exposing all the night of man
That soars throughout the heavens far above
Illuminating all that taste her hand.
A stone am I and yet I feel her touch
That burns within me- turns me into sand
A desperate fire eating at my heart
Because I will not ever join her van.
She flickers in the night and turns from me
Then seems to slip away toward other lands
How longingly I stretch to grasp her light
Knowing within my heart I never can.
She shows me her starlight for which I yearn-
All dreams of holding her forever burned.

Where is the Light?

Where is the light?
When I close my eyes to the world,
Where is the light?
Does it shine in spite of me, or does it die with my empathy.
Frail, weak & useless
I stand among the collective humanities–
For a time I studied them,
Looking for their causes
Trying to understand
Wanting to aid them
Needing to feel that I had tried.
Now I look at their outstretched hands & see my own
Their tattered rags are the remnants of my life cast away
It worries me that in trying to help, I hurt.
That reaching out to calm, I caused greater grief.
I despair at the prospect
Afraid now that I can offer nothing
Cringing, I withdraw my hand & return it to my pocket.
I step away & let my focus leave their desolate eyes
I stiffen slightly to their cold emotion
Then slouch in indifferent resignation
Disturbed, I suffer one last glance
Then shut my eyes & welcome darkness
Their haunting specters frozen in my mind
Memory
Cold Darkness
& Night
The dark unending night of the tortured soul.

Beginnings

Out of the Depths of the Darkness
Out of the Caverns of my soul
Primeval & Menacing
Arose the echoes of my past
Foreboding they towered around me
Darkly encompassing my mind
Etched with the faces of names long forgotten
Deeds & Locations known only to time
I stood in awe
Gazing in wonder at images of myself
projected sporadically on unknown locations long past
Fear crept into my heart
gathering the reins of my soul
slowly, silently, structuring my sensibilities
seeking mastery of my memory
A voice cries to me in the darkness
reaching in from light beyond my hearing
"There is no past
All you are viewing is in your imagination.
You exist from the time of your birth
Through the time of your death.
The same holds true for all humanity–
Each an isolated mind closed to access by any other
Except through their window of experience."

Noble & Still

Noble and still
Lying with eyes closed
raised above the seated viewers
half concealed within a silver casket
oblivious to all surrounding
Hale and composed
Unfettered by illness, duty or care
Features sternly set
A delicate curl in her hair
Eighty-nine years brushed away
Eight years of decline fortified
An image created
successfully representing soul and spirit
A grandmother long forgotten living
remembered dead
Strength required
presented in weakness
Family architect
Reset as matriarch
Dissolute members
regrouped as family
Faces unknown
Names decades forgotten
Regained & reinstalled
in memories fading
In fear approached
In warmth, sympathy & comprehension retreating
A delicate passage
From life through death and beyond
Each molding renewed existence from sorrow
Begun in Hell
Communally purged
In Heaven completed

Furious Dreams

Darkly my soul resides
In shadowed depths unknown
Inside the hidden crevices
I hide – hoping
Sounds await
Lurking outside my silence
I dream
Furious dreams
Untethered, uncharted
Long into the night
Beyond the screams
Beyond the sharpened arrows of conscious conscience
Untimely wind
Nearing oblivion
Sunken in long remembered torment
Smoke ridden
In fire tested
Golden truth
Sleep forever in the dawnless night
Sleep & dream

A Walk With You

A walk with you
Down the avenue
Down the tree-lined path
Over this gentle hill and that glorious meadow
Under the summer sky
Awake to the life of the world
Alone in our dream
Together in our nirvana
Sweet summer smells
Arise
Wafting with dandelion pollen
and rippling heat
Across the face of the world
Tickling the grass like the delicate hair on your arm
Soft to the touch
Your silent voice my only conscious sensation
Your graceful movements the rhythm of my soul.
Hand in hand through the trees
their shadowed arches
a welcome canopy
Leading us deeper into their mysteries
Above the clouds gaze silently down
In textured pillows of white & gold
Vast blue expanse
Light filtering through
A spotlight more splendid than any human imitation
Refracted into streams of light
Spreading out from their source
A look
A smile
All understood
We walk together
Slowly, silently, we melt into the countryside
becoming one in nature.
I look in your eyes & feel love
I listen to your gentle breath & taste hope
Cradling your arm I am strengthened
With tears welling I turn away
and lead you on

Scents reawaken
Birds sing
the sun setting slowly over the horizon
signs its approval in magnificent shades of violet & flame orange
Every turn offers new beauty
Every stone leads us on toward new dreams,
New landscapes, unfolding new wonders—
And nothing more wonderful
than experiencing everything
Arm in Arm
Together in friendship.

Lust

Kiss me now
I love you
Drop all pretense and hold me
We are alone
But can be one.
Slip inside my arms
and taste my longing
Dream with me of forbidden things
And yield to the temptation.
I tire of excuses
and abuses
It is time to act
To lunge after my desires
to acquire the happiness eluding me.
I want you
Now
I need you
Always
I love you
Dearly
Madly
Uncontrollably
Undeniably
Hold me
Kiss me
Today

In Silence Sleeping

All the world in silence sleeping
While inside my heart is weeping
Lonely calls to quiet shadows
Longing for the peace the night knows
Turning, hoping, thinking, dreaming
Touching, wishing, inking feeling
But oh the peace that floods the soul
When fitting parts into the whole
My aching heart no solace knows
Except in dreams that come and go
Each brings joy then dashes hope
Leaving scars with which I cope
Silence and Darkness my only friends
Sustain me when I sense no end
And just when fear seems most pronounced
A sudden change helps me rebound.
A soothing voice and gentle presence
Give life to lungs in need of essence
Restoring strength thought dead and gone
She heals, revives, and passes on.

Touch

Reach out
Spread forth those glorious arms
Extend those delicate digits
Like Michelangelo's God
Touch
The gentle pressure
Slowly radiating from that simple sense
Rushing through these rough-hewn limbs
Brings life
Awakens the soul
A hint of love
Wafting across the stifled air
Inhaled
Tickles the fancy
Descending head
Leaving eyes & mouth corners riveted upwards
Creates the devilish grin you see
An impulse takes root
Movement ensues
And the buffering distance evaporates
Pause
Regard
And slowly raise a restless limb
Slightly quivering in anticipation
Reaching out
Returning
Touch

I Walk in Silence

I walk in silence
Beside a gentle stream
Its noiseless current flowing
over rocks still calls to me
It lingers 'neath a solemn cliff
In awe I do the same
Then it starts into a darkened wood
and soundless breathes my name

Awake to Spring

With the wind wafts
the sweet liquor scent of spring
All blossoms in bloom
on this breezy afternoon
Gentle rising currents
Carrying with them hope and the spirit of life
An intoxicating consumptive
at the repeal of winter
The dark, soulless days of captivation
Break swiftly apart and dissipate in the refreshing air
I slept in hibernating silence
Coiled, lifeless inside
Balanced between restraint and decay
Seeing no end, sensing no release
Until the growing light touched my nose
and suggested resurrection
In weakened, stilted movements I arose
and crept forth to drink the beauty in
Tired and lifeless I continued
Curious about the source of my strength
Undaunted by fatigue and the resistance of my body.
With each step I confidently straightened
And entered, wide-eyed, beauty I yearned to grasp.
With unproclaimed suddenness
My soul leapt toward the sky
Reined in to its container
It stretched toward its goal
Drawing matter into spirit
Gone all traces of the night
Replaced with straining effort to take flight
And kiss the very face of God
In rising crescendo
of rebirth and revitalization.

In Love

I am in love.
I see you across the room
and my heart races to embrace you
I close my eyes to still the beating
and sense you following the change
I stretch my mind to read your thoughts
But mystery surrounds them
Shrouding their secrets
behind a wall of innocent behavior
and acceptability
You pass near
and I bask in the wake of your presence
Electrified I dare to dream
But catch my leaping heart
before it escapes my chest

Wonder

What color are the leaves in your eyes?
I see yellows, reds, much green
Some sparsely covered trees,
Some still fully laden

Does the sky look blue to you?
I see white clouds dance across an azure floor
Serenaded by the rustling leaves
Invigorated by the sun's strobe
of white and gold
Long orange sunsets
framed with pinkish sky

Dazzling Day
draws to a close
leaving me in wonder—
wondering how the world looks to you

Flourescent Dreams

Psychedelic color filled motion
drifts across my conscious mind
unconsciously
I revel in the display
as I am swept along the flood
where I am going
I know not
nor care
Only hope in desperation
my destiny lies there.
Tired roaming weekend fears
surround me in my waking moments
weakening resolve
and teasing my imagination with fanciful delights
Aaaaiiieee!
In mixing horror/fascination
comes the penultimate climax
pounding nerves
and greasy drumming fingers
keep the pulse flowing
jumping with anxious movement
through the night
through the day
Into the evolving time of memory
and glowing shards untouched
and untended
erupting on occasion
into flames

Lord, Touch My Heart

Lord, touch my heart
and let me walk again
So many paths remain for me to trek
So many smiling faces yet to meet.

These days are long and lonely
Weary isolated vacant hallways
echoing with mingled hope and despair
A frightened child I willingly become
and lift a wavering prayer

Lord, touch my heart
free it from the cold clutches of dark thoughts
Give me the strength not just to stand
But to stride
Fill my weakened veins with meaning
and let me walk to your purpose

Whisper

Whisper softly
to my delight
I read all details
in your eyes
Wind whistling gently
makes me smile
I'll linger awhile

Breath sweet with love
awakens my sleeping soul
And promises new hopes
New Dreams
New Love
to chase away my bile
I'll linger awhile

One hollow echo
reminds me of the past
Intruding briefly
on my solitude
Awakened layers
of sense and sentiment
come fast
and wash me through
with joy
and hope
and aching tender
threads of love
that sustain me every mile
I'll linger awhile

Weakness

Weak of will I wandered
Through a maze of misconception
Spread my cheer for all to hear
Who smiled to see me coming
Now the days of joy grow short
As winter falls upon the soul
Shoots of spring are left exposed
And wither at the sudden frost
My fears are confirmed
All hope is lost
The silent shelter of the forest
Has become the pillared hall of death
Entombing me within
There are no ghosts to haunt me
No loved ones, no enemies
All thought, feeling and action
Have deserted me
And I stand in silence
Waiting

Down

Down through the forest
Runs the quick little brook
To the foot of this hill and that
As it makes its journey
Toward the lake past the farm
It gathers and widens till fat
Through the fields now it wanders
with no place to go
Feeding farm after farm with its touch
On its surface I drift
with its current my guide
And await what will come of my luck

Blue

Low and gentle blows the silent wind
stirring hope and healing aching wounds
There's a scent of joy that wafts on wings
held graciously aloft on careful strings

Touching hearts it makes its steady way
from man to woman and back throughout the day
Here bringing quiet cheer, there taking it away
Enveloping arms enfold each as it may

Carry me to the ceiling of the sky
to brush and touch the face of eternity
fill my soul with sweet enticing lies
then sweep me down to join the ill at ease

Wholeness comes through steady contemplation
Heart with heart, soul with mind, imagination
spread with contact through the human nation
in final glory unifies the grand equation

Skyward

Skyward, ever skyward
Let my eyes lift up
While the wind infuses my spirit
With strength and lifts my wings
Like a seagull on the shore
Waiting for the right gust of wind
To pick it straight up off the sand
And let it beat its way.

Skyward, ever skyward
Let my mind take wing
Gaze up and out
Through and beyond
To words and feelings
left for me to thrill among
across the universe

Upward, ever upward
Into the open air
Until I brush the face of eternity
Drink in its essence and descend
Swooping to earth intoxicated
with life, love and liberty

She Stands Alone

She stands alone
Raised above the crowd
Strong and resilient
Steel-cold and pure
And she is loved
Her court has been cast
her suitors spent
She has drawn her circle tight around her
And through it all
Unknowing
She is loved
Once joined in merry song
we danced our dreams away
And now the night has closed upon our mirth
She stands apart
But not in my heart
For through light and dark
She is loved
Unseen behind a shroud I stare
and revel in the vision fair
While she blooms in the midday air
Though cold should grip her
Where she stands
And leave her with an empty hand
Forever proudly she will stand
Unbent before the wind
For she is loved.

This One's For You

Warm in the night
A subtle movement
Unseen, unheard
But sensed all the same
is felt
Across all time
its presence you could gauge
Running my fingers along your spine
Tracing your shoulder blades
From arm to arm
Drawing a gentle pressure
up your outstretched calf
with dexterous toes
And smoothing nervous knots
out of your tender torso
The warm breath of
eye-shut darkness breathes
its soothing power on your
outstretched neck
Pulls every heartache
free from bonds
And brings love to
the deepest, most forsaken
corner of your soul
This penetrating warmth
heals wounds long open
erases scars long held
And fills you through the days
to come with utter bliss.

The Rarest Flower

The rarest flower withers at first sight
Its beauty lost to interpretation
Turning to dust before both eyes have seen it
I've witnessed this in person
With barely-reined excitement I turned to
drink in the nectar of a glorious blossom
In one instant I was blinded with untold beauty
which touched the epicenter of my heart
and sent it leaping to the stars
My mind evaporated into time
My body into space
My soul became one with the universe
And before my vision was restored
the delicate petal had turned to dust
and been blown into uncertain memory
I only recall the most beautiful words I've ever read
The sweetest taste ever to pass my lips
the bluest sky, the greenest grass
the deepest eyes I've ever lost myself within
For an instant we were one
then beauty vanished in a sudden gust
And I was left standing still
in stunned silence
Left only with that imprint on my mind's eye
To carry me to my life's end.

On a Dreamy Day

It is a dreamy day
Slow and easy
Warm and hazy
Tired arms prop
tired heads
While eyes look away
living through the window
in a distant sky
the radio keeps in stride
with its soothing strains
and paints a background serenade
Minute by minute
the time slips away

Drifting overhead
across oceans
of water and trees
Carried on in silence
by a summer breeze
To a distant rendezvous
on a distant strand
There to smile
inside my heart
While reaching
for your hand

Waiting

Standing in the dark
with only time to ease my mind
an empty building
is my silent companion
But I match it silence
Standing, waiting
Free to speak
Free to say what ears can't hear
What words don't form
When light or eager faces
Stand and hover by your side
Alone within a timeless world
Where minutes drift with hours
past cold, gray sentries
Not giving any heed
And leaning in the dark with
Racing mind
And turbulent unconscious
I strain to think of what to say
and what to do
and where I want to go
And when, and how
And always with who
But the wheels only spin
as the night disappears
paying silent farewell
to me and my endless
Waiting

Tender Thoughts

Tender thoughts keep me going
How I'll hold your hand
Cup your resting head within my arm
Send you silent signals with my eyes
But I also feel the pain you suffer
See the anxious looks and grimace to myself
Watch the lines draw down your face
grow deeper, longer
These moments age my heart
And tear my soul to shreds
For if by some slight touch
I could mend the tear
Slow the wear
I'd reach out and
Brush against your side
Take you in my eager arms
And flash a healing smile
To see warmth
Return to every part of you.

Daydreaming

Some things in life cannot be matched
the scent of freshly mown grass
The cool taste of a summer breeze
The songs of birds on a lazy afternoon
the warm kiss of a high sun
And all the memories of your face
Scattered through my mind
I've stared entranced while spring leaves dance
upon a steady breeze
Spent hours waiting for one cloud to leave the sky
Smiled with bare emotion at the world coming to life
Before my eyes
Sent my soul fluttering after yellow butterflies
across the lawn
or you slipping down the stairs and out of view
Peace of mind comes hard
And not with effort, but with patience
So too the pieces of your heart
So sweet the reward
Yet oh, so long the road
But nothing makes the passing sweeter
than watching the summer day drift by

Rain

What is life
Without a little rain
A summer shower
To wash away all cares
And ease the daily strain
To soften my sadness
Refresh a tired step
Bathe the world with tonic
To right it on its way again
A misty night across the beach
Arms entwined beneath the damping drops
A seaward gaze into forever
Reflected in your eyes
Then home to dry before a fire
Long into the pitter-pattered frame of night
With thoughts of love and warmth
Until the glowing embers wane

From the Mountain

Today we'll climb a mountain
stretch out upon the rock
And lie together spinning dreams
for the world spread out below
The wind will be our messenger
Carrying whispered desires to our ears
And taking finely crafted hope
Back to eager waiting souls
the thrill of timeless love
will be our pleasure
As we weave our afternoon
of sunlit gold away
Each gust suggests a new direction
as it brings shivers up my spine
Each impulse leads to further beauty
And another reason to stay here with you

Sharing the Moon

Alone in the wonderful cool of evening
I close my eyes and breathe the night air
A brief stroll with the breeze at my side
And a hint of light through the trees
My attention is drawn to the sky
Where clouds part to reveal a glimpse
of the moon in all its splendor
Shining its face to mine
I gaze into its radiant face
It speaks to me in silence
No words fill my ears
only the sound of the trees whispering
No - the moon speaks to me inside my heart
While my eyes hold its glow in a steady gaze
The words come unheard, but certain
Whispering promises of life and love
And I have to smile to hear their charm
for they come addressed to me
the words are directives to my heart
And I listen eagerly for their instruction
Hearing all that comes to me
I smile for joy and happiness
Knowing that same glorious visage
Shines into your eyes
Peering out from another cloud
Leading your heart to dream of love.
And I smile a second time
While waiting for a third

I Have Searched Within

I have searched within
Laid out my soul and studied
every piece, every part,
until I knew each element by heart
And recognized its presence by its touch

Some are rough to touch
Some smooth, some pleasant
all different, and worn
each with its story attached
And none too small to play its part

But what do they unite to form
What whole is made up of these parts?
And what effect would moving this piece there have?
Or switching that with this?

I cannot see the answer
And there is no one to consult
to solve the riddle
or save the day
or bring order to the chaos

But for now I do not care
I see the pieces and appreciate their beauty
I move them as I can
And learn what I can
Against the day when
Decisions must be made

For Now

Summertime stirs the soul
Warm sun, cool breezes
Hours gazing into the afternoon sky
watching distant clouds drift slowly by
Keeping all the beauty of the world
locked tightly in my silent mind
For now

Watching waves caress a twilight beach
gently smoothing ripples from the fading day
erasing all evidence of its heated passage
with cool, damp sand and soft scents of the sea
bringing rhythmic peace with growing darkness
to a heart locked tight with hidden grief
For now

Across Tomorrow

Wide eyes open to an unknown world
A distant time
and years left behind us
in the past
Memories wash over tired hearts and minds
Stirring pleasant thoughts
and starting shallow dreams of reopened hope
Long into the tomorrows
My eyes search, looking for
an easy road
a place to rest or enjoy the view
But all I see are rocks
and broken bridges
Dark, cavernous maws
and reasons to stay put
But my feet have always been restless
and I also see the water flowing
over those rocks
Hear the crash as it breaks
down the mountain
and carries it to gentle folk
content down the bed in the valleys
I see new trees sprouting
From among the broken pieces
of old wood
Catch the faint scent of wildflowers
and summer dew rising out of the darkness
and ache the more to enter
Caught by the moment
I sigh and settle back
Content for now with observation
and appreciation
But the sadness still lies deep within
and listens to the music of the wild
calling out for me to join its chorus
And I strain my mind to
hold my eager body-spirit at bay
No trails to blaze today

But knowing
There's another day waiting behind this one
and a stretch of tomorrows
losing themselves in the distance
swallowed up by shadows
and the forest walls
So like the mountain now I'm strong
But waiting for the call
to be revived
and saving strength to make the journey last

Firelight

Distant snow topped peaks
Flicker on the inside of my eyelids
Teasing me with lusty dreams
of quiet nights and tender warmth
Firelight, rugs and eternity with you
Waiting for the stars to cross the sky
Writing our time away with care
Touching the root of emotion
in the pure air
cold and sharp
met with a wind that has run free for hundreds of miles
Just to brush against our faces
And sweep on to the next midnight dreamer
Hiding down the valley in their own corner of perfection
Nothing breaks the darkness
But the lights above
And the orange flickering flame reflected in your eager eyes
We can stand here in the night forever
looking out upon our world
Savoring each eye-catching moment
Hand in hand
or take a moment to test the inner measure
of our private space
Stir the embers on the hearth
and drink a different beauty deeply
till the sun brings gentle reminders of time and other things
Then roll awake and taste another day

The River

Drifting throughout the days
Down the wide expanse of time
Warming to the climbing sun
Listening to each sound that lights upon us
Birds dart overhead
Silhouetted against a pale blue sky
The heat keeps us still
And the current pulls us along
on the distant shores
the trees reach out to us
Eager in their own way
to ride the waters to another shore
But we care not where we are led
only hold the moment in our minds
until the next one rides in on the wind
Someday soon the water will reach the sea
And everything lazy and beautiful
will be met with a pulsing sea
that could swallow us up
Unless we can weather the impact
Pull ourselves to shore and safety -
But for now the dreamy clouds
Wafting overhead
Suffice
and fill the hours of the day
with casual hope and peace of mind
Elusive and distant unless we ride together
Hand in hand

The Touch

In the darkness a hand reaches out
slowly sliding across an uncertain distance
searching for something to touch
But what does it find…

Will the fingers trace the outline of gentle face
forgotten by the faded light of day?
Will they meet a waiting hand and share a blissful
moment together in the shadows?
Will they find a supple neck-line to trace from
ear to collarbone?
A firm-skinned arm tense with restraint?
A thigh taught with sinews eager to pull bodies together?
The small of a shirtless back teased with the sweat of the day
and weeks of anticipation?
The long lines burrowing into sleepless eyes calling
through the hours for the coming caress?
The growing pounding rising heartbeat stirring in
a heaving, breathing chest?

The fingers slide with eager hope until they meet
returning fingers reaching through the darkness
from a silent presence searching on its own
for fingers, arms and skin to weave their magic on.

Beginning Again

Sorrow grows in silent strains
Touching deep chords of the heart
Sadness is my song today
And plays itself through my veins
Alone I sit in quiet contemplation
Waiting for my muse to call
Waiting for some inspiration
But no words come
The voices silent watch with me
As the sun settles in the west
And emptiness floods over me
The song I wish to sing has no words
The words I know carry no tune
The composer of my heart lies sleeping
Drained of spirit I sit and weaken
Splintering and wilting under steady pressure
and the dull ache of fading dreams

Brush

When I look into the empty sky
and dream your face before me
I have to smile and cock my head
Your breath falls heavily on mine
and my eyes sag behind their lids
While a well of emotion rising from my chest
floods up into my swelling head
And in the instant I am gone
Down roads longer than eternity
Standing, turning on the top of the world
Gazing out at everything in wonder
beauty and unbridled love
the ocean rises to my feet
and tastes the tips of my toes
with lapping laughter that sends my soul
singing into a run along the padded strand
Soon the ground beneath my winged feet
is lined with knee-high grass
and daisies, black-eyed susans, and buttercups
Red and yellow paintbrushes
all waving their delicate danger in the summer breeze
It brings me to my knees
I stop and gasp for breath
Consumed with overwhelming joy
and unspeakable happiness
the picture nearly perfect
Waiting only for the one touch I have missed
So I pause to feel the marvel of your kiss
And snap awake to light
And cars before me
or an empty white wall
teasing me with visions of paradise
And leaving a gut-wrenching longing
pulsing through my aching body
From every nerve driven point upon my body
to every drunken synapse in my mind
So sweet a moment
come and gone
A flash in fading memory
all of an instant long
But heartache lingering forever

Hours upon hours
Aching, yearning, lingering
Growing until a cloud congeals before me
and a face forms in the milky mass
leaning in to drive the drought away
And in the instant I am swayed
Cock my neck and tilt my head
with smiling eyes and lips now flushing red
tasting with the wellspring of emotion
A million blushing bursts of pleasure
leaning in to brush their lips to mine
One blip in time

Walk

I must have walked a mile today
though the greatest stretch of ground
was never more than fifty feet or so
But I crossed it and I crossed it
Back and forth so many times.
It was the only way to ease my mind
And it worked as long as I kept moving
Restless, ever restless and uncomfortable
Sitting, rising, pacing – thinking
Starting, stopping – always waiting
Waiting for the night to come
Waiting for the moon to call
Waiting for the coming storm
Waiting for the rainbow
Waiting for the pot of gold
Bracing for the wounds, the pain
The uncertainty and burning rain
the shadows and seductive gain
Knowing nothing will come easily
Knowing nothing may come at all
Still consumed with the enchanting call
Too twisted in my mind to see the truth
the agony and heartbreak and the loss of youth
Wounds too great to ever heal
Only caught up in how I feel
So I walk at least a mile a day
Back and forth across the room
Down the drive and back again
Never getting far away
Never finding the words I need to say

Pretty Eyes and Pretty Smiles

In the heat and humid air
I lie back without a care
all alone and thinking of the world
Pretty eyes and pretty smiles
Laughter welling in a child
Simple pleasures blissfully unfurled
No regrets and no remorse
Come to sway me from my course
So I sit relaxed and let the world go by
Waiting for a love so strong
it will vanquish every wrong
And lift my willing wings into the sky.

In the Darkness

Alone in the darkness I reach out
to run my outstretched fingers up your waiting leg
Look with longing to your eyes
And squeeze your hand for warmth
Let my index finger find the hollow behind your ear
Trace the line of kisses I will give
along your neck
across your shoulder
down your collarbone
just under your outstretched jaw
Then I brush my face against yours
My rough whiskers polishing your stone-smooth visage
Two strong sensations flare
the most special of which is the smile
that lights my dreaming face
From ear to ear
And wakes me from my silent reverie
Content with the pleasant knowledge
the dreams will never end

A Walk in the Park

A walk in the park
A few quiet moments
apart from the world
Living a dream
under the newborn summer sun
Eyes stretch skyward
to embrace the universe
and freedom of the sky above
Great arching boughs of oak
and maple stand silent against the blue
Shielding the earth from the sun
under their majestic canopies
Across the blue-white wall of clouds
a pigeon wings its flight
a seagull soars into the gaping blue
and carries me with it to other worlds
Upon the shaded ground beneath
Only the wind stirs the pleasant scene
and the frantic scurrying of a horde of squirrels
Smiles grow fuller all around
as the chest wells up with bursting joy
and brief tender moments
work their wonder
and their magic
on a heart grown cold and gray
Bringing peace and joy and comfort
to a thirsty soul
at the fading close of day

Sudden Impulse

On a sudden impulse
a hand reaches out
and brushes a suggestion
Willing eyes turn
startled with accepting impact
and draw more deeply of the well
How cold and clear the water
newly sprung out from the spring
It shocks with pleasure
and perfect refreshment
And is drawn on frequently
and ever deeper
for the rejuvenating,
reviving, power it contains
And for hours upon hours
one tiny drop sustains
Until the eye turns
back to draw on love again

A Warm Thought

Time opens its arms to receive us all
Corrals us ever deeper into its thrall
And all along the way
With every passing day
Our defenses wear thin
Letting cold dampness in
Until death makes its claim on our souls

Yet as we journey on our way
Toward that future bleak and gray
Together we can stand
Whatever comes at hand
Arm and arm against the night
With a love both strong and bright
Providing each other the warmth to make us whole

Memory

I remember now,
Lean in again
And let me whisper
In your hidden ear
A word, or phrase
That doesn't mean a thing
Let me catch that faintest whiff again
Of your hair stirring the summer air
Feel the welcome heat of contact
With your brushing arm
I remember now
Why that neck is so enticing
Let me near that line of flesh again
And I'll show you another use for a silver tongue
With a subtle tip along an inch or so
I remember now
Where my vision flees
When I close my dreamy eyes
And draw a sharp slow breath in deeply
Lips upon imagined shoulders
Fingertips lightly tracing love lines
Down a tensing leg
I remember now
Which way to cock my head
To meet perfectly in the middle
How to run my cheek against yours
And fall into paradise
One luscious passionate touch at a time

Do you remember now?

Sun Child

Eyes of the earth
With hair of fading gold
Alone against the backdrop of eternity
And verdant fields of summer hope
Tall and proud
Strong and unwavering
The sun child stands
Alone

Waiting in the scorching summer sun
Through long hours of oppressive heat
Holding steadfastly to his firm belief
That in the end his inner strength will prevail
In the end his heart will chase its course
And free his aching limbs
To hold and love again
For just as long as time can last
Against whatever storm may pass
Stronger in love than left alone
The sun child waits
Ready

Clouds

Clouds roll across the sky
Beautiful
Big, white
Thick and full
Billowing up like emotions
swelling within my chest
Luscious and soft
Like scoops of ice cream
waiting for the touch of your tongue
waiting for the melting warmth of your gaze
the slow spreading heat of your palm
the comfort of your head on my shoulder
Time slips away
Lost in the moment
Lost in the drifting clouds
Floating like dreams over a waking world
Carrying visions of night to open eyes
Drawing me toward you across the expanse
Knowing the miles that separate us
mean nothing to the heavens –
that the clouds that show me their left face
regale you with their right
I can only smile in your direction
and hope you catch the reflection
playing off the clouds above
I know your smile is there
It makes the white more brilliant
the sky a richer blue
And the love within your heart
drips from the clouds above
into my dreamy eyes
fills my longing heart
and satisfies my thirsty lips
If I could step into the sky
to wrap my arms around
the fluffy white
I would
in hopes my arms would fall on yours
reaching around the stuff of your dreams
Then we could drift together
above the earth

pure and bright
chasing day into the night
wrapped within each other
tight

Dark Eyes

Dark eyes showing
Bright with life
Strong in their conviction
Giving more than they observe
Teased with slow dances
played in silent winks and smiles
So soothing to my damaged soul
My whole body goes silent
almost catatonic
drawing deeply of the power
in those eyes
Dancing in time
in my mind
Rising, offering an outstretched hand
and twirling away the hours until forever
to the gentle rhythm of a quickening pulse
While time takes its toll in reality
on a motionless dreamer
stuck in his drifting pursuit
Awash in beauty, love, and empty strength

Delicate Dance

Words that dance like welcome music on my ears
Tease my mind through sweet, drifting hours
With tastes, and smells, and easy gentle sensations
of cool skin against warm skin, arm against back,
leg over leg, bodies entwined in one movement
of passion and experience, drowning time in a tight embrace
Suggestions visit my exposed skin through sliding fingers
and clutching toes, legs treading water
and my tickling tongue visits each in turn with a delicate answer
Drawn slowly along while hours slip away
Tracing promises of the night and coming days
Across an exposed belly taught with nervous reception
Each contact imagined is subtly suggested
and oh, so eagerly, enacted
While hands soothe aching shoulders, necks and backs
so weary from disuse and restraint
In happiness relieved and smoothed away
one touch eliminates, one touch invigorates
How does this affect your lower back and legs?
Do they benefit from the tender massage
and come to vibrant life?
The years peel away, the hours fly by
the strength of love returns strong and certain
to wake long-sleeping limbs, muscles and tastes –
and warm cold bones with the warm blood of love.

On the Breeze

On the Breeze
Still and quiet with the noontime sun
Warm and lazy under a pale blue sky
Listening to the sound of memories fluttering by
on the wings of a lilting breeze

Alone with the universe
And civilization a step away
Alone with the voices of eternity dancing through the trees
playing their notes on rustling leaves
Singing their songs of passion to me
While I sit back and smile,
laughter in my heart
and soft thoughts on my mind

Comfort holds me in my place
keeps this look stuck on my face
plays my heart with melodies tender and sweet
Fills my head with images divine
and my soul with words I long to speak
But in the stillness of the afternoon,
who will hear them?

Tomorrow's dreamer,
listening close,
will catch them
wafting on the breeze

The Voice

The voice
that cries its heart out
for all the world to hear
Spreading love and joy
Peace and hope
Dispelling care and fear
It rings out to the open world
Above the trees and fields
It rings out to the distant hills
Clear and unconcealed
The morning lends its growing light
to warm the ears that hear
the noon sun sends its brilliant beams
to stay their foolish fears
the evening bends its fading glow
to draw the willing listeners near
That songs of love
sprung from the heart
And sung out loud and clear
will work their way
into every soul
and be treasured there and dear

First Kiss

For many days I've dreamed of this moment
played it through over and over in my head
different angles, words, movements –
all ending in the same manner,
with lips together, eyes closed, in silence.

For me the dream ends there,
whether because it becomes too real to imagine,
or too thrilling to continue,
I cannot say.
Only that the moment our lips meet,
all linear time ceases,
and we only emerge from the contact
with some distant tug of reality –
the phone rings, the door opens, someone speaks,
or screams, or a car flies by,
so many moments,
with so many distractions to stay their influence.

There is nothing like the first encounter,
the pent-up passion,
barely restrained,
tearing at every part of your being –
the sudden final yielding
which melts distance, time and barriers,
leaving only flesh with flesh,
in precious lingering union

Let us bottle that emotion
and keep it safe against malaise
despair, and slowing moves of longing
as they fade with passing time
to age and still retain the splendor of the first touch
to grow wiser, stronger and more attuned to each other
while keeping the wild, unchecked passion
and carefree abandon of the initial press
of tender flesh to willing flesh
of yearning heart to longing soul
the simple strain of open feeling
that binds two drifting, dreaming minds
and in one vision makes both whole

Words

Many years, many months, many days
more hours than can be imagined
yielding page after page of thought and emotion
Written, typed, written and typed -
and more than a few spoken once for all eternity.
The treasured ones have fallen on loving ears,
good and bad, for better or worse,
and spent, they slip into the emptiness of memory
most slide by without incident,
without enough meaning to carry them on in the mind
But there are enough that speak the soul,
that carry hopes and dreams from inside my head
into the waiting ears of someone looking for their promises
These bring me greater pleasure than any written down.
They work their magic, and dissipate into the ether
remembered only as they are heard,
and as they are intended to be heard.
They leave no ambiguity of meaning,
for every reader to interpret as their own.
These words carry their message from my heart to yours,
and linger only where they are needed and desired.
The words I inscribe here,
and in my journals,
are shadows of the reality I can speak,
I can whisper in your ear
with closed eyes
and pressing silence
and only the warmth of our closeness
to light the corridors of our souls
and sing the music of our pleasure
and nothing to mark the thought
but fading memory
holding meaning as close and fresh
as desire powers it to do
My desire is to hold these precious words
close to my heart and fresh in my mind
for many, many years to come,
hoping for eternity to keep them true.

Once Upon a Time

There are special moments in every life
We brave the storms of everyday existence
on the wistful wings of promised joy
And certainly as rain will fall
These passionate times will erupt.
Many things happen in this world by chance
But many more speak to some design
All the little pieces seem to fall in step
of their own accord
but the whole that they complete is too clear
to be explained by anything but fate.
Wounds heal, tired eyes and heart and souls
find rest and rejuvenation
As the ocean rolls away, so it returns on the next tide
Choices made are done with all the best in mind
But often there are choices made for us
the job you can't refuse
the eyes that steal your heart
against all your better reason
There is a place for fairy tales and movies
and given the dream, how can anyone refuse
I long for the day my dreams arrive
that I may scoop them into my arms
and wing my happy way into forever
with the taste of utter pleasure always at my side

Showers of Life

With a rush of energy
Defying explanation
and overwhelming in scope
the sound cascades upon us
from every direction
simultaneously
Down through the leaves
and branches
up across the lawn
and underbrush
Fed by and feeding the
pulsing rain
falling freely
out of a wide-open sky
Crashing to the ground
around us and over us
In a deafening roar
that grows and deepens
threatening to lift our souls
to the sky
And wing our dreams
Into the heavens
and out across the world
long into the expanding horizon
or simply filling our bodies
with unlimited energy
to stand, to walk, to live
through daily tests that
stretch our comprehension
and drain our spirits

Sweetness and Light

For the first time in over a month
the skies opened wide
and rain poured down from heaven
over all the waiting world
Earth dry and cracked
drew deeply of the water
Leaves cackled with their rippling glee
the wind whipped around through every opening
Stirring branch and heart alike with energy
Invigorating and inspiring
the moments passed like magic
in the air – through spinning time
and left the mouth with sweetness
clinging to the tongue

After night had claimed its place
and the sun behind its watershield
had set into the distant west
After the water from the clouds
had spent its diligent course
I walked into the darkness
and for an instant I was stilled
I came abruptly to a halt
and let my eyes rise to the cloudless sky above
the sky once filled with clouds and rain
had given way to an abundance of light
Spreading from horizon to horizon
It struck then as odd
that for the month without any rain
the skies were clear and bright by day
And clouded over gray by night
The stars, if any showed, were dim and far between
Even the moon made only two brief token appearances
yet in the aftermath of day-long soaking rain
the clouds rolled back to show
the splendor of the universe
How wondrous to taste the rain and see the stars
to drink the needed moisture in
then look into the glistening sky
and longingly drink again.

Lips

Lips full and bright
tender, yielding
supple and fresh

Warm body present
holding still, caressing
enfolding me with love

Eyes always watching
drinking, giving
sparkling in the light

Ears perk up at any motion
waiting, hoping
listening for the next wave

Legs limp and numb
weaker from a touch than any exercise
strain to keep afoot

A smiling face
quivering and flushed
looks with eager anticipation

Waiting for a hand to quell the nerves
A kiss to seal the passion of the moment
And strong arms to steady through the storms

To stand together
no longer alone
and taste the joy of oneness

Held long into the night
the visions play easily
and bring their magic to willing hearts

Lips full and bright
teasing, tasting
sealing love in with a kiss

Basin

Picture of Perfection
Clouds hung low
All the world was shrouded in fog
the sea was like a pain of glass
Apart from two frogs, a fish,
and the picture of you in my mind
I was alone
Standing in the twilight on an exposed rock face
Staring out over the still, calm ocean
Listening to the strains of the radio
Singing my thoughts out to you
"You can call me a fool,
I only want to be with you"
Smiling I walked back to my car
leaned on the roof and let the music
fill my heart as well as my ears
You were all that was missing
Everything lay still and silent
Waiting for our touch to grant existence
to bring the spark of life
to awaken the sleeping beauties
I could have stood there all night
With my eyes closed to see you
standing before me
With my eyes open to see
the world stretch out before us
To take your hand and climb down
the rocks to sit on the shore
To cross the mud flats and tumbled boulders
in dreamy exploration
To sit right on top of the hill
holding hands or holding bodies
while the darkness grew deeper all around
In the cool night air
Against your side
Strong in our unity
Warm in our hearts

Tenderness

A quiet look in a sad moment
a gentle touch that washes away
the slow wearing strain of each passing day
a smile from across the room
that shines through any darkness
across any distance
to light upon my eyes

A soft whisper that barely tickles my ear
laughter that ripples through every room
wakes sleeping minds to joy
a shoulder to rest on
strong arms to catch you
if ever you should fall

A willing hand when strength ebbs away
a gentle word from an angry mind
a loving gesture from an aching heart
hope in the face of insurmountable odds
kept alive in a silent, caring heart

Remarkable

Indelible
Permanently etched into my memory
warm thoughts
long imagined
thoroughly enjoyed
personified in your presence
leave me thinking
you're remarkable

Eyes that sparkle without any light
hair that cradles your head in the absence of my hand
arms that reach out naturally to mine
draw me in
without signal or alarm
to stir the embers of my soul
to hold me in their charm
locked down and safe from harm

Without a word
you speak your mind
without a sound
you listen to mine
for hours upon hours
you keep me within your touch
hanging on your every action
waiting for another chance to say
you're remarkable

In my eyes
and in my heart
from every sinew of my being
radiating from every pore
spreads the wonder, amazement,
and utter joy
that is my essence
when I share my life with you

To me, that is remarkable.

Stars and Moons

Warm summer night
sticky and close
a thousand crickets singing to themselves
Dusk settles slowly
and the stars peep through
the gray curtain of the sky
With a smile for childhood
I picked the first I saw
and made a wish
Filled with a flood of memories
and emotion I paused in silence
stared into the vast expanse
and dreamed of distant planets,
stars and moons waiting
for contact
When we look into the night sky
and dream of holding the stars in our hands,
do they gaze down at us longing to be held?

The Beauty I Love

I can feel the moment
sense it deep within my body
wrapped around my heart
folded through my muscles and veins
stretching with each movement
Reawakening the wonder of expression
again and again and again
Each blade of grass
calls out to me
Each branch on every tree
the lapping water on every rock
the crickets and birds sing to me
the stars wink in understanding
the darkness enfolds me like a glove
the world I know is at peace
and I am constantly aglow
with each touch, each taste
each sight, smell or sound
I hear the laughter of nature
cascading loud and strong
singing to me of daylight
whispering to me of nighttime
And in each face, each hand
a memory – warm, thoughtful and free
Purifying, restoring, reminding me
that my world is not my own
My life is a borrowed life
Swiftly running its course
And the track that leads me on
reveals wonders all its own
Each turn yields something unexpected
Each day brings something new
Each moment leaves an impression
But all the loveliest are of you
In this leaf, in that flower,
In all the clouds that roll above
Are displayed for all the world to enjoy
the beauty that I love

Brown Eyes

Brown-eyed & beautiful
Warm skinned & smooth to the touch
Whistling in the night air
to distant stars
carrying a tune of the heart
to worlds shining in the night sky
Walking in the moonlight
Carefree and full of life
Casting spells on the sleeping world around
Spells of love and healing
Words of joy and exuberance
Touching every living stalk with beauty
Streaming from her soul
leaving heartprints on the watching world
And with delicate fingers
tracing dreams of fancy
across a night full of promise
hope and bright happiness

Salt of the Sea

Today
for the first time
I set my feet into the waves
tasted sea salt
as it crashed over my head
Today
for the first time
I dared the surf and current's pull
to feel the ocean
lick my head
Into the cold water
bracing for the impact
bobbing with the swells
Under the warmth
of a September afternoon sun
smiling
always smiling
wishing for the answering smile
in my head
Eager to wade in again
eager to feel the water
move my body again
Eager to crawl over exposed rocks
to a vantage point above the surf
to sit and listen to the magic
of the pounding sea
against the cliff beneath my feet
Not alone in the moment
not alone in the solitude of the music
Maybe to watch a sunset
or an afternoon drift away
or even an hour
under the full moon
with nothing on my mind
but the sound of the waves
crashing against rocks and sand
and the lingering taste of dreams
in my soul
Today
and everyday

Snow Flower

Pristine and bright
the snow flower shines
through the darkest night
across unmeasured miles
to my waiting eye
With the imagined scent
of its blossom clinging
to my nose
I close my eyes
and will myself within its petals
to drink the nectar
of its pollen
and feel the silken
touch of it against my flesh
Drifting through forever
with the warmth of its life
wrapped around my silent body
open to its charm
entranced with its beauty
and drawn to its touch
I slip free from timid steps
and stride the span of time
won over to its love

Leaves

Leaves gold and orange fill the trees
holding on for one more day
Knowing another week will see them fall
And in the low long light of sunset
in the half-light air of dusk
They glow with unchecked radiance
In a passionate display
That sets my soul on fire
Wishing I could fly
take wing and soar across
the vast expanse of forest
Drinking in the beauty of the world

But in the fullness of the day
the image of your face
outlined by your smile
lights up every corner of my mind
and wings my heart
across the distance of our lives
and sings to me the glorious
beauty of you filling my world

A tender smile erupts across my face
and swells to consume my entire body
leaving weary thoughts prostrate on the floor
While the joy within me soars
One moment beyond all sight and sound
full of tenderness and love
and only you beneath
to bring my flight back down

Orange, Red and Golden Yellow leaves
Cast fireworks upon my eager eyes
and fill the promise of my heart
that even passing time holds
many special beauties to embrace
Each new and wondrous in its way
And you within my heart
The most wondrous one of all

On the Rocks

The muffled roar of the ocean
the gentle constancy of the wind
the casual indifference of sea birds
drifting lazily on the rising/sinking sea
Alone with two thoughts on my mind
the pounding inside my head
and the longing for you in my heart

The white waves crash in rhythm
against the tumbled rocks on which I sit
their foam reaches skyward
while my tired eyes stretch out across the expanse
looking at the miles of open sea
distant islands, lighthouses, lobster boats
and at the silent stillness of the stone beneath my feet
and the shape of your heart chiseled in its surface
gnawing at the one within my breast

All my love and life are slipping away
while I drown in the overwhelming tide of the world
sitting lonely, cold and helpless
waiting to be pulled out to sea
envying the birds their patience and buoyant disregard
for the danger of the ocean beneath them
and tasting the salt of my tears with the spray

The Call of Summer Days

The distant call of summer days
has faded in the cooling evening
Snow-peaked mountaintops
Calling to my heart and soul
The warm breeze rushing through
Close-growing branches
of pine and oak
filling my once-weary feet
with purpose and direction
Have gone silent in the night
and rustle only as a grim reminder
of bleak, winter days ahead
But in the corners of my mind
the image still stands clear
With brilliant sky of blue
White billowing clouds
and all the open hope of time
Still calling me
still drawing me into action
still flooding my willing veins
With the rush and promise
of adventure
and rebirth
My silence is only surface-deep
Within, my spirit
Soars free
Cherishing the beauty of life
Storing it all for wintry days
and the memory of a summer smile

Prove the Wings of Love

Breathe the cold air in
Deeply
Hold it for as long as possible
Exhale
Repeat
Cast your joy-filled eyes into the heavens
Feast them on the shining stars
indifferent to our measured time
Let their seeming permanence
fill your reservoir of youth
and spring lightly on your way
Carefree
Rejuvenated
Lunge into the shadows of the night
Chase away the demons with the darkness
Grow warm in the expression of life
Action
Spurred by nameless passions
Deep within the vibrant heart
Taking flight to test the wings of love
in the thin air of life
Hold steady for a moment
Gather strength
Then breathe the cold air in again
Hold it till your lungs burst
Exhale
And soar into the beautiful world
To prove the wings of love
To beat a path into the stars' eternity

Inside a Restless Mind

Clinging vines of restlessness
Wrap around me
in the shadows of my mind
With dread encroaching
I sink within the walls of my existence
shore up my defenses
and wait the coming storm
In the angry wind
I cling to my sanity
and wish silently for respite
calm days and soft light
For in the empty silence
I can clearly hear my muse
Rise from ashes of indifference
and stride among the demons of my soul
Listen to the world that greets me
Hear the voices on the wind
See the faces in the stars
Taste the beauty of a quiet minute
and the elegance of eternity
Without condition I can open my heart
and pour out the feeling
I have pent up for too long
explore the marvelous nature of life
and warm myself in the glow
of welcome words
graciously received
by the moonlit night

Colors

Yellow
Daffodils and buttercups
dandelions
waving in the spring breeze
Tempting me to run
Barefoot and laughing
through the newborn grass
Red
roses and tulips
strawberries
warm and bright beneath the summer sun
Luring me to taste their joy
and pause to draw their beauty in
one scent, one sweet, subtle lick at a time
Orange
Leaves and pumpkins
woolen caps
starkly contrasting a world of brown
Free my lungs to breathe
the sharp air in
Unbound and uncontained
White
clouds and snow
Christmas
cold and dim beneath the low-set sun
locking me within myself
to sleep until the days are lengthened
and the bud of spring is reborn within my soul

Poised

Restless in the night
bracing inwardly against the cold
looking out at stars and silent trees
swaying in the moonlit air
and letting the conscious mind wander
to warm fields, and summer days
conjuring the magic of a simple touch
tracing beauty in the daylight,
one long embrace
remembered in the corners of the frigid mind
never fading from the clarity of passion
in which it was first beheld
the silent hunter waits
poised within his solitude
letting the luscious flavor
of memory run through every fiber
savoring the impact of emotion on the soul
content only with the simplicity of love
that held anxiety away
The night seems long and dark
but the quiet, elegant beauty of the moon
redeems the spirit from despair
and lets the warmth of passing time
awaken the senses of the soul
to themselves and the universe

Whisper to the Silence

Whisper to the silence
Let it know you care
Whisper to the silence
when no one is there
Tell it of your secret dreams
Fill its void with hope
Then when days are dark and gray
with silence you can cope
Bright sun shines on happy smiles
Blue skies reign when times are gay
But shadowed night brings emptiness
and shrouds the brightest ray
only in the quiet stillness
smiling at an unseen world
can the strength of life in loss
be majestically unfurled
Listen for the soothing moments
Between the anxious noises of the day
Take heart that when the world looks bleakest
The silence has a lot to say
Words I know so thoroughly
I can quote them as they're read
Words that give my soul a promise
drawn from the message in my head.

Memory of a Kiss

I can taste your lips
remember the line of your neck
as I brush your hair away
to taste your cheek
feel the movement in your eyes
as you arch yourself in invitation
smell the scent of natural beauty
as I brush against your hair
feel the strength of our passion
as we pull together
Remember the absence of time
and the presence of us
I can hear the low moans
and taste your soft lips.

Searching for Peace

I am searching for peace
inner peace
and can only sense it
in moments of silence
and solitude
I only sense disorder,
chaos, endless consciousness –
Never rest or relaxation
No rejuvenating periods
I only sense tension and unease
But in the absence of sound
I hear beauty
in the serenity of solitude
I can hear my voice
I can feel my heart beating
I can feel the wind blow
Taste the colors of the rainbow
Learn the cadence of reality
instead of the noise of life,
of living.
Night brings its veil to me
Cloaks the agonies of my sanity
in the fabric of dreams
and the whimsy of imagination.
I can feel strength in my wings
But I fear dawn
bringing its loud herald to me
stunning my senses
and inhibiting my reason
So instead of soaring in my
moments of strength,
I coil into myself
defensively bracing for
the first sound of the world
intruding on my soul
So I am always weak
and never really alone,
always accompanied by my demons

Soul Searching

It is night, and I am alone
considering the light
and the mystery of love.
Some days seem bright and easy
but hours passing
quickly turn anticipated pleasure
to maddening despair.
I am torn to pieces
with misunderstanding
and uncertainty
I can't tell light from dark
day from night
Hope from despair
Jubilation from terror
I no longer visit the moon as my muse
I no longer yearn for dreams
to entertain me
I court disaster out of longing
wonder at my weakness
and look with darting earnest
for some source of strength.
How long will I search before I act?

Morning Light

Night has loosed its grip
Moon, stars, the silent chill
have all faded into dull oblivion
In the bitter dawn
the air is damp and heavy
the clouds low and gray
the sky pale with the hidden sunlight
drifting beyond comprehension
only its filtered presence felt
Minutes tick away
and only the hands of time shift
Tomorrow will come to fill this void
but in the agonizing hours till it does,
Nothing raises the corners of my mouth,
and fear settles in
that one day will slip into another
without anyone even noticing,
and it will always be today
Until time passes away

The Call of Tomorrow

In my eyes the world is new
Bright in a way I cannot describe
It is quiet with a silence I feel in my soul
There is no anger, no bitterness –
But a faint scent of hope tickling my senses
Curling a smile onto my face
With a subtle twist
I will look to the stars
and recall their glow
I will close my eyes
and let the images burned into my mind
dance with me into my dreams
The welcome arms of sleep await
And tomorrow calls to me through the night,
tomorrow to restore beauty to a waiting world.

Quick Laughs

It's a hollow existence
Quick laughs
Subtle smiles
then awkward silence
straight faces
and a sullen shift to different corners
waiting for the day to slip away
Such precious time!
Willed away with fear, trepidation,
the cautious whims of moral safety.
The cool, flirtatious ease
of the conversation dance
replaced with shifty, downward stares
and the empty solitude
of life and love
turned inward.
Always hoping tomorrow will be better,
Always knowing yesterday is gone,
And scared to think the opposite is true.
Loneliness fills the void
between the empty words
and delicate glances.
Where friendship was once planted,
discomfort is now shared.

Beneath the Moon

Calm has settled on my body
listening to the rhythmic peeping night
Seeing the pale glow of the moon
edging toward full
So many months have passed since
I last looked to the night with wonder
somewhere I lost all hope
all joy, and let my soul sink
But in these quiet moments I remember
Sand in the night
the full moon clear and bright
time standing still
hand in hand with eternity
and I recall a smile
that will never fade
though I gray and crumple
the memory will stay strong
and keep my heart alive
give my soul hope to fly on
and plant the seeds of dreams within me
that will only grow at night
beneath the silvery moon

Dream Power

Keep the dream alive
whether it seems to be achievable
or fading
Never let the passion die in your heart
Dreams show themselves
in everything we do
in everyone we meet
But they are not confined
to what we do or see
they are vibrant and expansive
working within us
and across humanity
to improve all of our lives
Our greatest value
is to channel those dreams
creatively and effectively
in every way we can.
What appears to be failure today
may be the seed of tomorrow's success.
Remember me in your dreams.
Remember your dreams.

Lost

Wind is an echo in my memory
Fields waving in the sun
real in their moment
real in their pleasure
distant to my eyes
I could enjoy the world again
but I won't
not because it won't offer me pleasure,
not because I couldn't enjoy the offering,
but because I do not want to enjoy it.
The world is bright
The trees call me,
The lanes and scents on the breeze –
But I have shut the window to my soul
and will content myself with dreams,
the view from inside,
and the impressed memories of joy I know.
I could be happy again,
but I am content as I am,
alone and cold.

Colors and Textures

Describe your mood
paint the color of your soul
the texture of your heart
listen to the rhythm of your mind
while youth holds you in its arms
Each day more color is drained from my world
Trees are still green,
the sky still blue,
but they are becoming dull and flat
the forest is one shade of green
the sky and clouds are becoming one pale mass
the wind that stirred my passion
in days gone past
cackles in my ear
only the night still beckons me
to its dark corners
and still places–
but not for inspiration–
it calls me to eternal sleep,
not death,
just the shallow breathing
of a non-existent life
I can only hear the gentle wind
screaming through my consciousness
I am in a losing fight
and worried I will give up
succumb to tearful dreams
and tire of each new day.
The only rest from life is death
and I do not want that rest.

Your Eyes

Without a word,
they hold me tight
warm and enlivened,
glowing within,
bubbling over.
Without words,
they burn me through,
etching your anger on my soul,
until my knees buckle,
and I fall –
still staring
Without words,
you pick me up,
turn my darkest moods away
while I remember why
I want to smile
why I look forward to tomorrow,
why tonight seems so real,
and yesterday has faded
with my anger,
my frustration,
and all the sorrow of my life.
Hold me until forever fades
close within your heart
let me see the beauty of your soul
until I die
shine through your eyes.

Bright Skies, Fading...

I can't remember when
the sun shone so brightly
the trees stood out so clearly
against the pale blue sky
Before my eyes
and inside my head
the clarity sparkled
and I was spell struck
It feels good to laugh again
to share a smile
and open heart
But there will always be
a hint of sadness
and a fading memory

Each of Us

Each of us knows our own night,
our own shadows
our own cold
Each of us breathes
the scents of life
the wonderful joys each day brings
and the sorrow of passing time.
Each of us fights our own fears,
our own demons,
and reaches our own destination
Each of us lives
our own life

Upstream

Life is a forest
Many roads – beautiful, shaded –
With just as many dead ends—
cliffs, bramble patches, disappearing paths.
There is so much to see,
and all of it a treasure to the eye and ear,
but not enough days to reach the end,
to explore the whole of its mysteries—
Now and again there is a babbling brook,
clear and life-giving
But followed to its source,
it yields a brackish swamp,
thickets of soft earth
and impenetrable shoots.
The closer you get to its source,
the more it pushes you away,
the more distant you become,
the less appealing the beauty
that drew you through the glades,
over rocks, up cascading threads of water
I have walked that road many times,
each with as great an enthusiasm—
always ending with the same disillusionment,
gradual frustration,
wet feet, scratched arms and legs,
and lost ideals

Mysteries

Far from the glowing night of civilization
under the broadened sky
darker and wider
open above the world
stars leap into sight
hold me in my steps
and draw me into
the mysteries of the universe
What seems small, constricted
under familiar circumstances
grows giant in new spaces
and spreads to fill the unconscious mind
as thoroughly as the conscious.
Everything seems more...
More vast, more bright, more deep—
more beautiful, more enduring.
Such moments, in life, are rare
and burn themselves indelibly into memory
where they will shine forever.

Acadia

Over hills, around curves,
up and down the land's beautiful face
we have traveled today
catching a glimpse of the eternal,
and the timeless majesty of the world around us,
Still I sit in uncertainty,
vacation before me,
knowing tomorrow work will go on,
but I will stay here.
Knowing another week will pass
before I return,
knowing I will walk into the unknown
when I return.
My life has changed,
and I must change or die.
Like the world I whisked myself through
over the past 48 hours,
still where it has been for thousands of years,
but wearing every change worn into it
over that time
showing only the face of this generation,
while the next one starts to carve its own face
The world, so beautiful, inspiring, and still in appearance,
is constantly shifting—
another month brings fall,
another three, winter—
I feel the same awaits me,
and I need to find the strength
to keep the promise of spring alive within me,
and the hope that it will bloom again

Idle Thought

Some days I have nothing to say.
It takes effort to write
I feel no inspiration
and resist the chore of
conjuring something
just to meet an arbitrary requirement.
Often, there is much more I want to say
than words to say it.
Everything crashes together,
and nothing comes of desire
More often, the words are there,
but on subjects I will not embrace—
For all my insistence,
I am still not open when I write,
although I do believe that caginess
about revealing my true thoughts
gives an edge to what I write.
It is merely a continuing nuisance,
one which will no doubt continue still,
just as it is today.
But there is nothing for me in the past,
and nothing I can see in the future.
My focus needs to be on watching,
making who I am ready
for what presents itself.
I cannot see any change
But it always comes
and I need to be braced to receive it,
otherwise I will surely collapse

Waiting in the Fog

I look into my crystal ball
and all I see is fog
A cloudy haze around my life
every choice misdirected and misspent
But I need to keep choosing
need to keep searching
for the life I want to live
Working toward a future I can live with
one that will bring me joy,
peace and happiness,
one that will warm me in my dotage
one that will keep my soul alive forever
Everything I see, or smell or breathe is beauty
until I open my eyes
to confusion and disarray,
responsibility and indecision,
treading carefully forward
while waiting for the fog to lift
I feel too much relief when the day is over
and not enough enthusiasm
when it is just beginning.
I must find wings for my desire
and a cloudless sky to soar in

Quiet

Quiet
So quiet it draws you in
leaning into the blackness
listening
listening for some sound of life,
a car, a cough, a splash,
even a howl or a scree
But there is only quiet,
and darkness so profound
you can feel your eyes swelling
stars are popping out of the sky
and every detail of the world
is etched in deepening lines of shadow
This is where the external world shuts down
and the inner life grows
All in quiet stillness
full of wonder,
full of awe

Just Breathe

Restless
Waiting
Breath held tightly
in fear
in anticipation
light dawning
brings a new world
the mystery lies in how new
stinging or soothing
anxious or calming
only discovery
unveils the mystery
until then
restless waiting
and the concerted effort
the concentration
on taking one breath
followed by another
holding the function of life
chief among all thought
Just breathe—
Greet the novelty when it appears,
but for now, just breathe.

Silent Strength

Sometimes silence is the right choice
let thoughts slide away
let words die on your lips
close your eyes to everything before them
and open ears and the heart
to the silence of the world
We all know pain
We all know loss
We all feel alone sometimes
And sometimes we need to be left alone
we need to absorb the solitude
and renew our lives
Tomorrow will come,
and bring with it a full slate of concerns
It is in silence that we awaken strength
and through strength,
we endure

Listen to the Night

Listen for the wind
listen for something
to stir your soul,
open your eyes to the world
and let it show you life again
Listen for the night sounds,
calling from the shadows
echoing the melancholy sound
of your heart within your chest
I will know life
I will know love
For tonight I'll close my eyes
and listen for them in my dreams

Smile Paint

Don't the stars amaze you
High above the world
steady and immobile in the night sky.
I am wonderstruck at their sight—
not that they aren't there every night,
not that they change, or vary
from day to day—
But they always stop me in my tracks,
draw my dreamy gaze aloft,
and work a smile across my face.
I wonder at their power,
their display of permanence—
I know they are balls of gas,
and someday will burn out,
but their lifespan so far exceeds my own
and they remain seemingly unchanged
through rain or snow, fog or moonless night.
The weather only veils their presence—
soon it passes, and the stars remain,
drawing eyes and souls to them,
painting smiles across the face of the world

Time to Rest

Wild and free
At home within myself
Listening to the sounds the world makes,
Laughter, singing, weeping, sighing,
Eager to grow, eager to develop,
Ready to act

It is time to rest.
Time to yield to the weariness,
Shut down, and let my body rebuild.
Tomorrow will brighten my life,
Just like today has,
Returning my smile

A New World Within

Easy to breathe
a head full of ideas
new words,
catch phrases,
and budding philosophies.

So many thoughts,
dancing across the mind –
conscious and unconscious,
some closed, some shared,
some bright,
many warm with memory
alive with the scent of hope.

Each day is new and bright,
challenging and daunting.
Each day brings new success,
and shadows of old failures,
worn deep within the fabric of the mind,
a pattern etched in the nature of our lives,
waiting to direct us,
or be redrawn

Picture in My Mind

Yesterday, the moon spoke to me of patience
tonight a cold, dismal rain
commands the air
I am secure in myself,
but I have needs,
I have wants, dreams
some days they shine clearly before me,
others, they are veiled by rain
When I close my eyes,
I picture perfection
painting the image in clear detail
every corner, every angle
until the image in my mind is real.
I listen to the movement of my love
I drink its flow throughout my mind,
then carry it into eternity
etched in my memory
crystal clear and deeply embedded
a bright world within my reality
and a sustaining life force
in the harsh climates
life provides for us.
I will survive,
I will succeed,
and I will always dream

Just Once

Just once,
to hold the night out
just once,
to open my eyes
just once,
when sleep is calling
Stop to hear the world
to feel the power of stillness
the wonder of time
Listen for the sound of love
carried on the wind
one word in the still night
one thought
falling from a thousand stars
one dream imagined
among a million dreamers
and just once,
one dream fulfilled

Private Thoughts

Many times I sit alone
a dark world lingering in the shadows around me,
just out of my reach,
held back by the faint light of a computer screen
I stare into the glowing pixels,
and let my mental eye turn inward
searching my heart and soul,
searching my memory and dreams
for who I am
looking to see what diamond lies encrusted in coal
wondering if today saw me make the right choices,
keep the right focus,
move in the right direction.
Often hearing a voice tsk-tsking advice
on where I went astray,
how I should have acted.
I feel a sadness knowing there is truth there,
but though I know today is full of errors,
I choose to focus on tomorrow,
to keep it from following the same pattern.
I have an ache in my heart that I cannot quell,
a longing that speaks continually to my spirit
It haunts me and hypnotizes me,
and I willingly surrender.
Some days I feel alone,
the wind doesn't howl,
the sun doesn't shine,
time exists, but doesn't pass or carry any meaning.
I am waiting for tomorrow,
knowing I should keep my eye on today,
letting my passion slip away,
and my dreams grow without supervision.
I close my eyes to moonlight on the open sea,
Silence fills my ears,
and peace my heart –
These days I know I can survive alone,
but I feel the pain of loss,

I know that everything I need in life
flows from within me,
but my heart beats out the solitary rhythm,
and all I see is one
I can survive alone,
but I want to live together.
Life brings me the greatest joy
when I can share it
But life is not a minute or a day,
it is decades spent learning, loving, growing,
sharing, reaping,
and most importantly,
sowing.
The harvest of my life will be great,
if I am diligent with planting in the springtime,
and nurturing through the summer.
Fall is my favorite time of year,
but I always look forward to winter

Dreaming, Drifting

Long hours
Staring into the face of eternity
swirling shapes
and distant images of
movement
always hinting at something
always suggesting more
lurking just beyond comprehension
triggering interest
and changing the view
constantly drawing me in
and around,
leading me away from myself,
and deeper within
opening the universe to me
and closing the past
dreaming, drifting,
drawn along

A Moment

She stopped,
and with a smile held my eye
For that moment
we were one
In my darkness
there came a light
low and steady
showing me the way to open air
with weak legs I stood
and stepped into the warmth
of her embrace—
wrapped up in her smiling face,
held tight within her heart,
caressed softly with her words,
and loved deeply in her eyes
For a moment
heaven came to me
and willingly I welcomed her
for a moment
that will last a lifetime
and a love to last
forever

Shine

Every night carries it's own reward—
another day slid away,
another day sliding closer
and a world of dreams between
lit by stars and fancy,
following the moon,
and the hidden passions of a resting soul

In the right eyes,
the faces of the world glow
casting the radiance of the heart within
into the world at large
It is caught in the unforced smile,
the playful words coughed in passing,
and the tenderness a distant look can hold

Messages shine clearly
against the darkness of a frantic world,
and reinvigorate every muscle,
every thought and emotion,
with just their ambient presence
and the implicit understanding they are responding
to the way the world glows for them
as much as their glow acts on the world,
Like chicken and egg,
the light and lit
shine as one

Time Passes

Time has passed
I opened my eyes to the world around me
and I discovered that I belonged in it.
My joy was boundless
my energy level skyrocketed
A hand reached out to mine,
and I let it bring me into freedom,
into life
Time has passed
I opened my eyes to the world and saw its beauty,
the laughter in a child's eyes,
the love in their sighs
and the need in their tears,
My heart began to beat—
I learned to love
and cry
Time has passed
I am alone
the hand that led me into the world
has let me go to discover it on my own
I felt a shudder through to my core.
Weak, I fell to my knees and prayed it wasn't true.
I agonized and wept
and stared into the void
looking for the past that had slipped away
Time is passing
I looked for despair and found strength
I looked for nothing and found everything
my life began again
the fog over my thinking receded with the dawn
Though the joi-de-vivre is suppressed,
though the heartbeat is tediously slow,
though the tears that come have changed their tone,
still my eyes are open
still the laughter lights upon the children's faces
still the pulse of life and love flows
The hand that picked me up
still reaches out to me,
to keep me company, to walk along with me

Time is passing
While I learn to live
and the river of strength spreads through me,
growing stronger, wider
leading me to the sea
Despair has fled, but melancholy remains
With time my self-esteem will chase that away
and I will smile within
Time will pass
and this time will be forgotten
Old lives, old loves, will disappear
Old wounds, old heartaches, will heal completely
But I will stand secure
And carry my body with yours,
hand in hand,
toward the future
Alive, alert, anticipating each day we face
Let time pass

It Was

It was perfect
holding you in my arms
leaning into your soft shoulder
while the world disappeared
and all we felt was happiness
When the night awakes
and the world is quiet
under a blanket of darkness
the soft hum of machinery
fading into the background of memory
I feel your eyes in mine,
your hands in my hands,
the movement of our souls
entwined in delicate embrace.
I speak your name in my thoughts,
and feel you hear it spoken in yours
I can press into your waiting arms
and find shelter from all of my storms
I want your arms around me,
to hold and be held while the wind blows,
while the sun shines,
through the winter, through the night,
through the days ahead
To hold my head against your shoulder for eternity
not needing to move, not wanting to leave,
with our hearts one within our breast
and time smiling on us
Will you take my hand tonight,
and walk with me?
Will you let me be your shelter,
let me warm your heart
the gentle way you have warmed mine?
Will you sink into forever with me,
one with one,
while the universe fades?
Will you join me in our perfect embrace?

Heartsong

Words rise within my mind
they come to me in moments of quiet
they come to me in the midst of noise
they speak of needs, desires, anger,
past, present, and future
In their voice I hear hope and longing,
but also sound council,
wisdom and the persuasive reason
of patience and understanding.

Today I felt despair kiss my soul
but I also heard the laughter of my heart
ring out with beauty and opportunity.
I feel alone,
but know I have within my heart
all the company I need,
And I am held in other's hearts
None of us is alone,
when we hold each other tightly
with our love,
in our hearts,
in our souls

Always

When will I be with you?
Always
How long will I love you?
Always
When will time be ours?
Always
While I live,
I will hold you in my heart,
beating strongly against my fears
living to love
learning to live
and with a cherished smile
for fond memories
fixed in my head,
not fading
or forgotten
I will begin again
to taste the best of life
to warm my heart
to the depth of the world
and let the flavor of our friendship
linger on our lips
and keep our hands held tightly together
always

Discovery

It was in the night I found myself
in the darkness
alone
staring blankly into an impenetrable wall
closing me in
depressing me.
I looked long and hard for a light,
and found none.
I let my eyes pierce the darkness
hoping for something,
anything,
to reach out to me
and save me from the unknown
Nothing came
It was when I paused
defeated
to rest
that I began to notice a light
a small flame,
weak, pale,
within my breast
I watched transfixed
as it slowly grew
fed on my spirit
fed on my fears
my longings,
my desires
and grew brightest on my dreams,
my hopes,
my aspirations.
Everything I dreaded was consumed in the blaze,
and everything I yearned for danced in the flame
but when I looked into my hand
it was empty
when I looked at my body
it was naked
when I looked into the world around me
I was alone

A Walk With You

Again I paused
and wondered
Then I felt the fullness of my heart
the pressure of my soul expanding
the pains of growth in my mind
and knew the source of my strength was within
knew the treasure of my life was in living
and felt a cool breeze
chase the last of my reservations away
In darkness,
my inner light sprang into life
and warmed my world
without a word

Snow Storm

In silence lies the world
under a thickening coat of snow
Alone in the darkness, I sit quietly
remembering nights from youth
watching the snow fall,
walking through the enchanted evening
letting the absolute beauty and silence
speak volumes to my eyes and soul
Tonight I hear the same voices,
just as wonderful as years ago,
calling to me with passionate power
nothing more than an incessant tug on my spirit.
In the core of my thoughts
I am concerned about a friend.
In the absolute stillness of this winter scene,
I am calm and at peace with myself—
as I often am in her presence—
but concerned for her...
Is she at peace?
Is she inspired by beauty and silence?
I wish she could know the wonder of this moment,
lost within the treasure of the storm
soul bright within
this white winter world
stirring passions filling her soul
while calm flows through her mind.
Perhaps if my spirit is filled with joy,
she will be able to find her own comfort
when she is near me
I would give any part of me to let her be whole
There is so much beauty in the world,
and so few moments to fully appreciate it,
that every second of this winter eve is precious
and therapeutic for my troubled soul
I know a beautiful song—
"Listen, the snow is falling, over there..."
sweet and dreamy,
dripping white silence on a deafening world
and teasing my heart with hope and prosperity,
spiritual prosperity
listen, the snow is falling, right here...

Last Words

What do you say when there are no words,
when you have a picture to describe,
but no voice to give it life?
How do you free your soul,
when everything that imprisons you
has been built with your own hands?
How do you free yourself from your troubles
when the opportunities you have to move on
are used to increase the weight of your burden?
Every day my decisions become more difficult to make,
and yet every day I dig my hole deeper,
rather than start filling it in.
I see that change is long and difficult,
and resign myself to avoiding it.
My life could be so much better,
but only if I work on improving it
instead of continuing its demise.
I assess my situation,
and feel there are too many obstacles
for me to act now,
but tomorrow there will be more,
and my chances for success slide further away.
My life has been a journey,
32 years in the making,
but I have only noticed the path I am on
over the last few years.
Only in noticing a path
have I begun to recognize the journey,
and the need to choose my way
into the future.
I am new to this desire,
and green about how to move,
but today is the day to begin.
Today is the day
to begin…

Tender Lips

She has tender lips
In the half-lit twilight
They swell before me
Shadowed and sublime
A chorus of birds
Twitter through dappled branches
Call & complement to my heart
She takes my hand
Reaching out of a swirling universe
To ground me in her eyes
The touch awakes my senses
And calms restless mind
We will be one
The light recedes
Into the cool darkness
Of an early summer eve.
Those tender lips close to mine
And all thought ceases
I thump in thunder
Pounding
Beat, beat, beat, beat
Sweet moment clearing slowly
To reveal the starlit beauty
Of the night belongs to her
And she belongs with me

A Natural Call

Nature calls me
When the light of day fades
Truth be told
She calls me always
But I hear her clearest
In the dimming light
She calls me
In the onshore breeze
In every lapping wave
Against the sand
She calls me
In the rolling surf
In the ripple of each wave
Crashing upon the sand
Stretching,
Ever stretching
To reach further
Only to fall back
Recede into the relentless tide
And try again
It is the rush of my soul
Played out in pulsating rhythms
Pushing, pressing,
Stretching for more
Being drawn back under
To begin again
Wondering if the tide is with me
Or pulling me back
Understanding
As I hear her call me again
That the pattern will repeat
Another wave will form

Spiderweb of Hope

He watched her fly
Soaring with the stars
And breathed in joy
With her, clinging to a
Spiderweb of hope
That she could see
The universe unfold
The way he dreamed
It could be
But he never let her know
He held the key
To her heart
Now grace is gone
And new winds blow
In the growing darkness
As clouds command the sky
She weaves through shadow
He still feels her joy
But it rides through him
Like a memory
Playing back
Of summer days
He feels her intense eyes
Catch him often
In her spiraling dance
Knowing she thinks of him

Blow Breeze

Perilous thoughts
Call me in the darkness
Temptations freely kiss
My unconscious mind
There's a tickle there
A trickle of thought
Bleeding through
Whispers released
From the shadows
Pent up behind walls all day
Grinning twisted dreams
Step out from propriety's cells
Freed in the moonlight
Dancing in the evening breeze
Walk into this darkness
Feel this shame
Scrape your vanity
Look beyond the hedge
Feel the pull of the ledge
The screaming crash of surf beneath
Stand at the edge of eternity
Consider the infinite
On the sea breeze
Breathe to the pulse of the tide
Fill your lungs with salted spray
Call your fantasy across the waves
Feel the rush of time
Break open to let the darkness in
Or maybe let it out
To dance with demons
While you dream
Where life meets love
All you want, you need
Presents itself to be indulged
Dance while you can
Remember how to be free

Think A Picture

Sometimes a picture
Paints itself in the imagination
Colors chasing ideas
Infusing them with feelings
How you draw on energy
Hold the moment in your hand
And let it draw itself
Words upon the page
Bleeding emotion into eternity
Staining time itself
With eternal now
Looking down
I see my hand is shaking
Or is it tears shaken
From my sobbing eyes
Ragged thoughts run jagged
Across the warping page
Tears dilute ink
All stain
Paper, skin, time, future
Tomorrow when dry
All the variant emotion
Lies set in place
Dried in a contorted aspect
Of what we felt
Thought or saw
Wretched distorted image of
Imagined future past
New dreams will follow
Sparking new tears
New ideas
And ever changing pictures
To present through time

Only Real If You Can Feel

Night begins with casual eyes
Smoldering across the room
She captures my gaze
And lures me to her
Wicked thoughts
Flickering inside
I am eager to please
So I acquiesce
She starts the dance
Pulls the strings
Unleashes heaven
With her whiplash sting
Binding me within her ring
Cackling madly
Baring a malicious grin
But you don't see her
How I see her
Behind the fire of her lash
Compassion fuels her drive
Every pain she brings
She kisses to heal
Every time we embrace
I feel the warmth
Beating in her heart
Touch me
Taste
Always feel–
Feeling real

Wordless Conversation

Her eyes say come to me
Mine raise in mild surprise
She drops her gaze
For just an instant,
Then intensely snaps back
Impatience in their stare
Mine drop demurely
Paying proper apology
I cross to take her in my arms
We try the dance floor
Hand to waist
The music fills us with movement
Now there's a conversation too
The night grows dimmer
Slowing as it stills
Soon hands guide hips
Toward the door
Seeking quiet, private halls
To let the conversation continue
With eyes still dancing
Fingers find their way
To moaning reminders
Of all our hearts say

She Moves Me

The way she came to me
Moving without moving
Gliding, floating
Who looks at her feet
When those eyes
Capture eternity in a glance
But there is always movement
She elevates my interest
And the temperature
In the room
"What do I do for you?"
My question stops her
Tilts her head to consider
Then she smiles
Unfocused hazel beams
Regain their laser sighting
Holding me riveted
"When I've crossed the next ten feet…
Tell me what you're going to do…"
I think she purred,
It may have been a growl
"I'm going to trace your curves
Head to toe."

Dive In

It is never enough to wade through love
To feel the ankle deep flows and current
Tickling your toes and cooling your feet
Love is a cannonball off the deep end
All in, full immersion, sinking into the depths
To feel everything – cold shock, warm currents,
Pressure hugging you tight, burning lungs
Aching to draw breath, but unwilling to leave lips
Locked in needed embrace
Surface for air, crawl out on the sunbaked rocks
Along the shore, explore everything and enjoy
Time is for learning where you want to be
And going there
Start with a full embrace
Dive in!

In the Wind

Wind blows cold
Through thin branches
And thick needles of pine
The whooshing rush
Accented with creaking groans
As tall brittle trees strain
Against the pressure
Soon their tips will bud
Broad leaves of green will
Spring from them to catch the breeze
Cushion the sway
And ease the trees
Aching spines
Their groaning aches
Transformed into gentle swaying
An expression of laughter and joy
Dancing in the wind
Subtle changes bring
Profound variation
In mood and expression
Put a smile on your face
And see how brilliantly
It lights up the world around you
Then dance in reflected light

Starlight Visions

Feel her from afar
Ripples of light
Over moonlit water
She sings of starlight, watch it
Dancing through her eyes
She is beauty
She is the spark
Let her pulse
Stagger me
Burn within like
Sunshine in our veins
I wake to her
With fire surging
Her breath on the wind
Stirs the growing flame
She comes to me with
Ice cubes & candles
Cooling touch
That turns to steam
Flickering light
That seals our bond
The piercing contact
That stings with freezing burn
Descending
Nerves on edge
Ignite with eager
Electricity
Rising frenzy
Quivers in the glow
Unshielded
Light pours
Ice melts, wax cools
Fire rages with the storm
She is the night
She sings of starlight
Taste the brilliance
Of her mind
As her soul coats mine

I am the preacher
Calling to eternity
Proclaiming love
As fires burn
For her

Through Shadows

Came in shadow
Cloaked in mystery
She called out in clear voice
Turning to respond
I felt the need
Two-headed beast
Saw it in her eyes
Felt it in my soul
We walked along
Trading thoughts
Learning who we were
While learning what we lacked
Always learning who we want to be
So it began

Some thoughts come simply
In the dead of night
Lying awake
With only your silent thoughts
To light your mind
And shadows fade
As an idea comes to play
Born of your heart
Its need
Its depths
Long dark and empty
Knowing it beats to heal
That hole that grows
Is your soul bleeding
Cautioned not to give so much
You see instead
That you are meant to give it all
To offer strength
For those who may not have any left
Let them call on you
Let them lean on you
Give them joy you want
Create the laughter you each want
By lighting their life
With the spark burning within you
So it began

She knew darkness
She knew despair
She was the eye of the hurricane
Being buffeted by each gust
Tearing at her fragile shell
She noticed something shining
And stepped out to say hello
I noticed and replied in kind
Two heads turned in one direction
Why doesn't matter
Only that the light came
And started the fire
Burning between them in the night
So it began

Long roads travel over varied terrain
Slow learning steps and direction
Careful tentative movement
Until the way is clear
The pace comfortable
The company perfect
We walk on
Through the everlasting night
Laughing as we can
Knowing dawn may never come
But with the glow sent off
From the spark burning within
We have all the light we need
To show us who we are
To lead us forward
Toward another day
For warmth when winds blow cold
For comfort in the storm
We pause as needed
For shelter as it rains
Or to linger with our thoughts
Listening to the song of time
Watching stars march
Into the past
While we wait
So it goes

There is sadness in the song
If we tarry very long
So we stand and carry on
Who knows for how long
Yet we are joy
Where only shadows dance
We are sunshine in each other's eyes
For each remaining day
I am content in your care
As we walk beyond midnight
You are comfort in my arms
As we consider
Tomorrow never knows
What hope our dreams hold
But together we will journey
Into the unknown
Arm in arm, soul to soul
We carry on
To find where we belong
So it begins anew

Ashes to the Wind

Princess of dawn
Spreads joy with light
She means the world to me
Sunshine of my love
I long for your embrace
There is magic in your touch
Like flame to coal
Ignite my soul
Scattered across time like
Ashes to the wind

Eternal Sunset

Sit beside me
On the front porch swing
There's a fading glow
In the western sky
And I'd love to see it
Reflected in your naked eye
So I can watch your evening smile

Sit beside me
Take my hand in yours
Let us close the day in silence
Watching orange fade to peach
Peach to streaks of gray
Stretching out far beyond our reach
We can sit forever in the twilight

Sit beside me
Waiting on a night that never comes
While we're here we'll laugh
Tomorrow can ride the endless rails
This sunset holds our hearts
With a glow that can never fail
While we hold it in our memory

Sit beside me
Let me stare into your eyes
While I read my latest poem
Feel the words caress your soul
Reaching deep within
They're meant to make you whole
One with the light fading into night

Sit beside me
In this eternal sunset
Sing with me to the shadows
Stretching out across the lawn
Our heaven lasts while we enjoy
Disappearing day's final yawn
Hands held warm, hearts beat strong

A Walk With You

Sit with me
While the light remains
Feel it sink into our souls
We'll never understand what tomorrow brings
So let it go and stay with me
We're done dealing with uncertain things
Sunset always shines within our hearts

Steamy and Dirty

Lights low, music playing
Shadows dancing on the walls
Her body flows to the sofa
His eyes studying her curves
Eyes dip as she pats the cushion
Willing him to join her
His breath escapes slowly
As he crosses to her side
"Not yet," she says
As he moves to pass her
Her hands steady his hips
He feels the heat of her palms
Through his jeans
The steady pressure of her grip
Trembling fingertips
Betraying their eagerness
His hand drops to her cheek
Cups the curve of her jaw
Tilts her head to hold his stare
Smiles reassure the sparkle in her eyes
His heart beams as her smile warms
Light from the fire pulsing
On her face like the rush of blood
Pounding through his veins
He kneels to still her lips with his
Moist need blending
Tongues parting lips to embrace
They kiss for one long breath
She unbuttons his shirt
While his hands massage her back
Finding their way to unhook her bra
She runs her fingers through the hair on his chest
With a deep slow moan
He tastes along her probing tongue
They part for air, his arms drawing hers up
Lifting shirt, bra, and arms to the sky
Leaving two behind on the sofa
Fingertips tracing down her arms and sides
To her waist

Her arms drop to his shoulders
Feeling their flex as he lifts her
Standing they find lips and hips
Swaying in the music to the firelight
She finds his belt and slips it free
Unbuttoned jeans stepped out of
Coil upon each other at their feet
She climbs on the sofa on her hands and knees
Tempting him with her stare and unsubtle pleas
Guiding him to stand before her
She tastes his approval of her every move
He looks down her pale skin
Shifting in the dancing shadows
Hands stroking down her sides
Feeling the breath drawn in and out
Resting on her rocking hips
As they roll with her attacking motion
He moans in the glory of it all
Mesmerized by the roll of her cheeks
One smack
Just to accentuate his enjoyment
He feels the snap of pleasure surge through her
Watching her cinch her knees under her
To raise that beautiful ass
Present it fully to his stinging reach
Soon his hands stop
To steady his balance
One on each cheek
Holding her open
Fingers learning a route
His tongue longs to follow
Parting lips, moist with desire
She pauses to roll over
Giving him access to drink of her dew
They are heat and motion
Moisture and desire
Squeezing and stinging slaps
Affectionately claiming each other
Until they turn to merge
Mouth to mouth
Groping, probing, pulling hands

Guiding hips to rock in rhythm
Sweet and hot
Finding and holding the sweet spot
Riding into their sunset
Hard and fast
Enjoying every moment
As though it was their last

Not Yet

I feel the weight of life
Pulling me down
I feel the weight of slipping time
Escaping my grasp
I feel the weight of eternity
Smothering me
My voice rebuffs them all
Not yet

Look at the sky
Overcast and gray
Look at the trees
Bowed at the coming rain
Look at the people
Bent to the ground
My soul screams against it
Not yet

So I stop for the roses
To fill my senses with hope
So I stop for the sunshine
To fill my heart with warmth
So I stop for the birdsong
To fill my soul with promise
Listen to the echo in my mind
Not yet

Take my hand for laughter
And dance
Take my hand for comfort
And cry
Take my hand forever
And breathe
If eternity calls your name
Not yet, reply, not yet

Shadows Dancing

Shadows play
Across the wall
Dancing eagerly
Licking
Flickering
With each crackle
Of the fire's flame
Watch and learn
Breathe slowly
Feel the sizzle and pop
Of each blistering crackle
Bodies moving in half light
Slow, jumping with each flicker
They join and bend
Tumble across the room
Finding each other
In so many different ways
Exploring those and looking for more
Two eager spirits
Wanting all they can find
And offer to be enjoyed
They play off each other
Laughing in joy
As they push all the boundaries
To become one
Finding in the moment
They are one in mind
And spirit
Joined in body
They consecrate their union

Chariot

Park your chariot, Princess
The night is young
Let's enjoy!

Mind Adrift

I feel myself adrift
Within my thoughts
I find peace in quiet moments
Where the stillness
Allows me to focus
I hold my body still
Listening to the ache
In joints and muscles
Staring into the glow
Of the monitor
With no thought disturbing
What to do? I wonder
No reply returns
There are poems I wish to write
There are tales I wish to tell
But I only feel the fan
And hear the clicking of my knees
She haunts me
I feel her eyes on my soul
As I try to paint words on the page
I'm too tired to struggle
So the effort is weak
But the floating sensation
Is strangely calming
And I ride its wave
Allowing the weight of work
And time and life
To fade around me
I will sleep
And invite the words
To visit my dreams

Listen to the Waves

Speak to me
With your actions
Speak the language of light
Through gripping
Darkness
Show me how you feel
How your internal joy
Ripples throughout the universe
Let me listen to the waves
As your conscience cries
Tears unstoppered
For joy or pain
Tracing memories
On your face
Let me kiss their passing
Heal you of your blame
Let me hold you
Through the storm
Or dancing
In the rain
Share the lasting night
Wrapped within my arms
Let me be there
For the dawning day

Awaken

Hidden worlds
Lie nestled within
Rigid forms
Of propriety & decorum
She dances for me there
A wispy fate
Lost in paradise
I pace gray avenues
With her song inside
Calling out to my soul
Come to me in still dreams
Lie with me
Under silky skies
Laced with sparkling stars
Awaken
To my touch
Feel the music
Flutter in your heart
Make light your feet & spin
Arm & arm
Through waving fields
Across the bounding crash
Of foaming surf
Dance & be free
Shatter form for freedom
Forever dancing
Here with me

His Kind Eyes

She moves with elegance
Through the days of her life
But finds herself drawn like the dawn
To his kind eyes

His kind eyes smile
When she looks his way
It lifts her heart at the start
Of each day

His kind eyes weep
In the quiet of the night
As they watch her daily fade
Slowly slipping away

His kind eyes always
Carry her spirit to the stars
Hold her tight to mirror her light
Now & always

She is lost in each instance
When she catches his eye
The rush of delight at the sight
Fills her with joy

His kind eyes invite
Her into his open arms
With the tug of a hug
Enfold her with love

His kind eyes remain
When hers close on the world
Head laid to rest on his chest
He weeps for her soul

His kind eyes fade
Without her approval
Though he knows how she glows
In his heart

Out of Shadows

Out of shadows
Shapes coalesce
First in fractured forms
That swirl before
My consciousness
But there among
The frayed vortex
Two eyes appear
Raven black
With longing & desire
They grasp at my emotion
Drawing form
From my need
Fixed by my eyes
Drifting toward me
Flaring with cold fire
Surrounded by smoky visions
That tease my lovesick soul
With their expressive dance
She takes form
Amid the frenzied energy
Erupting in the wake of
Sizzling stares
A tentative touch
My sin

Rhythm & Groove

Feel it
Umm
Feel it smooth
Feel it slot
Into a groove
Ride the rail
Ride it true
Match the rhythm
Pounding through
Find that pace
Let it race
Let the blood
Rush to your face
Ride the rail through the night
Subtle shifting slots it right
Feel the rhythm rock your core
Taste delight & beg for more

Tame that...

Paint Me a Home

Paint me a home
For my heart
Show me the care
You give it to live in
Let me see
What love looks like
Through your eyes
Are there roses in the yard?
What color are the walls?
Walk me through
The layout
Hand in hand
Show me where
Our hearts will rest
Where they'll play
Where they'll curl in comfort
At the close of day
Paint me a kitchen
Bright with light
With laughter ringing
Off the walls
Shade it in hope
For the years to come
Then listen with me
Till midnight calls
Paint it clearly
But not completely
Leave room for details
We can make together
Painting it our own

Bathed In Light

Two halves of a soul
Matched pairs of the whole
Swirling through the
Depths of the night
They dance eternally
Through the conscience
Through the cosmos
Stirring in darkness
A seed of one
Growing in the other
As light burns to shine
It is overwhelmed
Wrapped in despair
Hidden
Compressed
Diminished
Only to spark
In the heart of darkness
Soon enveloped
Bathed in light
Beyond measure
So consumer is consumed
Light fades to shadow
Darkness gives way to light
Broken hearts
Bleed out their anguish
To fill anew

Feed the Beast

My touch is light
But you'll feel it deeply
The darkness grows
Long minutes stretching
Inside lies hunger
Appetites awakened
Yearning to feed
The low rumble of need
Churning for release
Makes you writhe
In eager anticipation
But I am the master
Marking time in my own way
Drawing your emotions out
To meet my stinging passion
Stretching out to play
Nimble fingers tinkering
Across your bristling flesh
Set your pulse exploding
Pressing at your breast
Heart brushed softly
Lays its desire wide
Lies exposed to view
An open invitation
To my secret weapon
The feather touch awakens
Your pleasure centers keen
As I descend upon your length
To stir each distant limb
Stroke the fire that lies within
Coax the burning feeling
To spread throughout
While I steady your pleading head
My careful slow approach
Eyes holding yours
In locking gaze
Leads whispers from my lips
To make you breathe
Breathe in my kiss
With pure joy in release

Knowing more touch follows soon
More brushes from my lips
And kneading magic fingertips
Can only heighten every sense
As your body sweats
Heart pounds to welcome all
And your spirit swells within
As you prepare for bliss